Saltire

the rythms of life poems

SK astro

/ BookLeaf
Publishing

India | USA | UK

Made with ❤ on the BookLeaf Publishing Platform
www.bookleafpub.in
www.bookleafpub.com

Dedication

dedicated to all who writes and loves poetry

and

to my family and friends who likes me and supports

Preface

The life has its own mysteries , twists and turns.The experiences which we gain through our journeys are treasures.

In our fast pace of life with busy schedules and technological leaps.Human relationships have become more materialistic.

These poems enquire about deep human nature and thoughts.

Acknowledgements

Love for poetry and writing came from my childhood.Great poets Wordsworth,Shelley and Gibran enriched my mind.

1. The journey

Journey starts from the seeds.
Man a traveller with inner sense .
The different journeys thee venture
With Fellow travellers having paths distinct.
Shadows as their soulmates
Follows them wherever they went.
Varied seasons and characters thee met.
The ventures they took.
Glorify them ,or can humble .
Donot go with the fellow
who like to trick you with his notions
Find the path which you make
It can be dusty,windy or muddy.
wade with courage and live the life.
Tales will unfolds, guides in the lively path.

2. Mysterious paths

Mystery!how poweful you are
Your name itself wonders many
My life told me you are my mystery
Your thoughts intrigued my paths.
Those paths were strange and windy
Knowing your unknown life
matured my mind,
The potion it flamed my sorrows
I tried to be you
But the course was of thorns and brittle ideas
defeated I felt, on reaching you
You gave me chances which I couldnot make
The dumbness in me argued,
They told that success is luck
My soul told me One day I will be
Falling to your power and wisdom.
Eventhough you were someone else.
And not wanting to know me anymore.

3. Faith and wisdom

The wizard told me, I am a fool
He mingles with his wife, the faith
Wisdom came to me
asked to join his hands of glory
Am I past time,I enquired myself
Faith in my mind felt silent
Wisdom fluttered his wings
And I touched his feathers
They asked me to fly
I looked at my hands ,
No wings ,me cried in despair!
You have to sew for yourself wisdom told.
Thoughts indulged on prayers of my soul.
Wizard again appeared
And asked me stand on my toes
To walk with pride
towards the eternal glory of life.

4. Marital life

The Life we sail together
Eventhough we are two souls
Commitments with different ends
Bound to be clothes to each other
Started our journey by joining hands.
Together we stood in the world arena,
Our souls mingled, thoughts unified
With varied outlooks in the physical world
From different backgrounds we came.
The high colourful dreams we started together
Not knowing the treacheries of life
Betrayals ,softquarrels,mutinies we face
From us come new lives
Who has to be nurtured,taught and grown
Time mightcome early to fell apart for some
For others it might be a bond to their end of life
Noone to be blamed,
Each pair in this world ,
has their own destiny.
Noone is a failure nor a success completely.

But world mark each of them differently.

5. Night life

Sat by the coffeeshop
Rich aroma wafting the nostrils
My eyes gazed upon a crowd
Cheering on a little girl
Violin she plays',
Dancing with her notes
The notes mesmerizes,
Changing to melancholy
To a sweet romantic tone.
Their moods changed like seasons
Farther corner ,her mother
Stern look on her face
Slight wrinkles ,a tin infront
Coins poured on tins.
Plain clothes neatly,
Anxious looks she had.
About the tomorrows to come.
By the brewing coffee ,my gaze went
Upon the rusty bar
Farther on west,

Bear cups clinking each other
With young men ,false romances
Lighting their faces ,
Young women as there cheers.
Trapeze on her feet,
Worn clothes ,poor.
Lushing the crowd.
Coffee on my table
Sipping lightly,bitterness
I felt ,my mind lurched.
The paved stones ,
Lighted me to a woman,
Greyed hair moving,
Wrinkled ,weatherd face
Her umbrella ,guides as her stick.
Uncertain of her path.
How the ages changed.
Phases they gone
Through the truths ,the falses
Their minds troubled and cherished.

6. Children

Who are more powerful
Children or men?
Men saw children innocent,
Children saw them as actors of real life .
Our ideas of life grew from childhood.
Some argued,others denied.
A toy in their hands I saw,
children were playing with the toy plane,
The garden they played.
Beside the fountains of purity.
Innocence paved their paths.
truth guided their minds.
When the machine flied in the skies
they argued to be its pilot.
First maturity came ,
when they chose
their Leader.
Some became his subjects and followers,
others fellow leaders
Friends,foes and lovers.

A world they created for
their play to be continued forever.

7. Passion and compassion

Oh , my passionate mind
have you ever encountered compassion!
Did your mind compelled your body to work?.
dedicate the time needed ,
for your soul to regenerate
Let your thoughts know you ,
guides the way which suits you.
Gain everything with a second or loose.
Sustain in passion and compassion.
Think of the betrayals you faced.
The faces around can deceive .
Even the eyes can lie .
Charm you with their compassion.
The shadows around can whisper their cries.
Reign over your emotions,
Read over others minds
to differentiate the passion and compassion,
of the crowd around you.

8. Ethics of nature

Oh,mother nature
How you reacts so swiftly
When our own homes are taken away
By harsh realities which encroach us
The water came in front of our gates
All at once,a night shower
Eroded our shores,the kins next to us
Swept away by your hands
Cries in our own souls
Fire oneday burned the trees
Smoke hung in air
Suffocates ,tore apart loved ones
Other day you trembled
the homes collapsed.

Is it our acts which angried
Or grief in our lies tired you.
The flora and fauna ,altered
From their habitats.
The scene viciously done.

Doomed are we now?
Or there is a chance for tomorrow!.

9. Love life

Love happened when I saw you
Your brown eyes and thin smile
told me ,You like me.
The first days we want to meet each other
Every other day.
We exchanged our glances
spoke of our thoughts silently.
Then came emotions of caring
liking each others opinions with respect.
Days of longing and despair
feeling aloof from crowd ,
where I once belonged.
Standing for each other,
even though we are paper boats
to stay afloat ,

Sometimes your emotionless face
noncaring nature
a better critic of my life.
making me be more bold

and strong even in the
middle of a storm.
You were getting through
the life.
The same passion we felt at once
didnot sustain at the same value.

Like the stars lighten the skies
Like rainbow rise near the clouds
Let the love of you and me
Brighten our life I wished.
Even in the departure,
at the end of the road
when we part as strangers.

10. The Apprentice

He was an apprentice
With high dreams,
was keen on his duties
A distant land he came from.
Even had difficult with language.
to express himself.
Truthful he felt to everybody.
Only mingled with highest in ranks.
But showed empathy to fellow's
They considered him as secretive
A man of mission.
Had the ability to subdue others.
The Cast of uncanny.
Obeyed the orders with precision
played the games none other can
Executive powers he gained
Made him more ruthless
But his men loved him.
glorified him of his presence
and dramatic nature.

Secrets he kept
made him the trusted vault
of the century.
The Apprentice, he was once.

11. Erratic Performers.

Performers with nonconsistence
Not able to succeeding in anything.
People remembered
Great were their deeds
But coulnot be greater in their life
Not gifted with riches
Players of streets they were
Best performers in life
Coulnot sustain every day.
Played every character with
Greatest strength they can muster.
Actors,actress.leader,lunatic,beggar
Rich,royal and everything
Shorter roles at different phases.
Not great parents.
Even though so much concerns.
Everyday they have to improve themselves.
To earn each day,eventhough gifted

12. Anger and Fiery words

I felt anger surging in me
Fiery words came from mouth,
They acted as if I am cruel
But the planning was treacherous
My words were harsh
Slipped tongue created havoc.
They took my riches.
wanted a confusion of mind.
The words once thrown
cannot be taken back.

And they waited for venegance.
The blood thirsty minds.
Once hurted with words
never reheal.
They want to torment me
by hurting my loved ones.
I donot want to be the pray.

My anticipation told me
to be quiet for some time
and to wait for the reply.
Reply came as actions
not as words.
I heard bullets at a distance
Sharpening of swords.
Me put deaf ears for a while.
And a blind eye.
To survive and to escape defeat.
and scandal.
I put my mouth to rest.

And to repent with actions
even though smarter ones
deployed for play.
Lost my own value,
Mind felt the despair.
My mind told me to put
the armour and helmet.
Take the shield
Or you will be the scapegoat.
or the gambit for the next event.

13. The battle of glorious

People watched in apprehension
The battle of glorious.
They were curious and enthusiastic
to watch their words,
to be the followers.
The words and letters,
became swords and sheilds.
Mutinies and backlashes gave way
to debates and discussions.
The country showed their love
to the leader in their votes.
They want to know ,
who is victorious.
Whom to follow.
It decided their future.
The truth and false
the lie and fake,
the business and economy,
the worship and faith
the actor and martyr

faced eachother
in the battlefield.
who will win ,
whom we can trust
every person looked
into the battle of glorious.

14. Royal relations

When we open our eyes
in the earth
relations come to see us
sometimes wishes goodluck
or badluck forever.
Best friends or worst enemies
not by our deeds
But by our birth.

The family compares
all the times of life
from childhood,adolescence
adulthood or even in the old ages.

When their stomachs are full
even with power of crowns
They mock at our empty stomachs
want the riches which we inherit.
They mingle with best

of our enemies
Always gives ear to
worst of our lives.

They use replicas of us
to adore them
cherish at our weakness.
Even our next progenies
fate is unknown.

The Royal relations
An eye or ear has to be silent.
forever
Words carefully crafted
Deeds keenly done.
or nothing can be undone..

15. The defeat and prayer

Am a soft minded soul
How I easily accepted defeat.
Defeat is a calculation of errors
accumulated over time.
A smarter one calculated the ways.
Fetched things better than you.
made you into a system which
he designed and reigned over you.

You accepted the defeat.
Prayer the anthem of life
tried to heal you.
But the power in you
felt the disgrace of acceptance.
You cannot blame on your thoughtlessness.
And irrevelant actions
which led to your defeat
The passage of time
which you can deploy better
have gone as a wind

which cannot come back
Smarter ways than your foe.
A system they created
Where you are the
complete stranger.

Oh soft minded soul
have you accepted the defeat!.

16. Fallen leaves

The winter came all of a sudden
With a short spring and autumn prior
Leaves couldnot understand
Why it came early.
Why we want to fall prematurely.
We coulnot see our unborn fruit.
The time might have elapsed
Or if the seasons changing rapidly.
Faster with the planetary motions.

Sky was very clear before
Now the vision fogged by thick mist.
Trees cannot see eachother for a while
The leaves started falling.
A long thick winter ,
Silence of the falling snow
The piercing cold into the barks
Of the trees.

Frozen lakes nearby

With small fishes playing
Underneath the thickice above.
The trees standing alone
Looking at their leaves in silence.
and despair at the,
fallen one's!.

17. Green fields

The breeze passed through the fields
As a small wave with a ripple
Whistling of the grained shoots with a fipple.
A humming bird with her sweet
fluttering of wings
And a nest hanging in the
tree top near.

A drizzle came next
with a drazzle.
dew drops hung over the leaves
shining with the morning rays.

The farmer woman passing
with a tone in the muddy path
The cranes flew near the
scarecrow
looking at me as a trespasser.

Frightening the children

who were laughing
and playing in the pond nearby.
The flowing stream
with her slow rythms

Then the sun bright and
hot,matured the grains
glow golden brown
to be harvested
with passing time

The festival of reaping
and people dancing to their steps
Joyous mood of love
and sweat gave a pleasant life.

Next time I passed ,
rolls of hay showed
the empty fields
lying with their bare vastness
all their grains grown
and gone

waiting for the next rains
and seeds to be sown.

18. The fame of unknown

One day unknown met the God
and asked the power to destroy
a place.
The place which want to twist
everything to anything
Mightiest of Ozymandiaz
lived there.

God didn't replied
smiled at the wishes.
When your soul rise
to Power of wisdom.
And your body met
with nettles of pain
I will give the chance.

She waited,defeated in her entire life
tortured by the cruellest of minds

Slept in the shadows of night.
Her fathers soul wept ,
the cry of he'll
and aroma of heaven
waited for them with their wings.

The Golden throne stood
with the kings shadow
The sword smiled
the trade told we want
to abandon you

Crown with jewels
doesnot want to stand for anyone
The fame of unknown
lived on the feet of throne.
Wings fluttered with angels
stood on the path.

19. The Investors mind

One day I met an orphan
How you grew up,I asked
A penny each day I made ,
for a pot of soup betted with many
walked in rain barefoot
In the Lamps of street studied
cried with empty belly
Noone heard the despair of life.

One day found a girl
who gave some coins
poor was she
not that looks she have
I feared if she have stolen it.
Investment started in small
turned to large
The girl left me after sometime.

20. Torture and pain

If you want to pain a person
Talk to them the worst moments in their life
always ,Make them regret
for the good deeds they did.

Make the mind of foe
into a cage of thoughts
And create a pseudoworld
with worst of her enemies.
Make their rivals to rule them.

If you want to do treachery to a person
Act as her lovers and wellwishers
And plan without involving her
till the end.
And tell against them only
when they are doomed.

If you want to disgrace a person
Show some respect in the beginning

And make yourself the trader above them.
And mourn in front of her
until she get disgraced by herself.
Make themselves fools who cannot
think above you.

Show sympathy when your enemy
fall down.Study the weakness.
And play the cards.

You cannot pain a mind
who has seen the world
to the right of the eyes.
and freed from all of the
chains which they are born.

21. The Double Gamers

Beware of the Guy
who smiled with you once
Dated with other the sameday,
Eventhough stranger
Acted as some one related.

Donot follow double gamers
They know how to pull their threads
You will be the person
to fall on the dungeons.

Your pride will be gone
When you go after someone
Who want you as a prey.

Its not the rich game
which will come first
But the game which seems easy
that cannot succeed
You are only made to play

As opponent player was decided earlier.

22. The solace of solitude's

Rolling over the years,
World remodelled itself many times.
Many seasons came and went,
Man evolved through
the technology.

Secrets of the world.
kept with some .
To sustain our race as humans.
Solace into their own solitude,
This question raised in minds.

Is it needed to attain peace.
The tranquility of time.
Their own lives in better societies
Makes happier lives
and future generation's.

There is no real truth in the world .
It's the time which changes

truth or false.
Every soul can turn good
after their bad deeds
Its repentance they say..

Be the famous mouths.
Of the society.
Only people hear from the fame.
Not the truth they wanted.

Money once gone from your hand
willnot come back.
The taken ones can keep
them more keenly.

Donot watch over men
They can take your time
and money,for knowing
their lives.

Solace in solitude
Thats what we gain in the end.

23. Rhythms

He played with rhythms.
Time changed its rhythms
Waves followed the same
World rhythm to chaos.
Heart beaten once
stopped its rhythm
took by pacemakers.

Machine opened its
bionic eyes.
Impulse rhythms
of electronic waves.
Kid looks at his
Chatbot, it showed
his likeable rhythms,
the stories and rhymes.

Quantum smiled at his
fellow chips,
the better guy I am,

The smarter rhythms.

Raindrops with it's shower
in natural rhythm to new lives.
The river with her currents
as music rhythms
to the sea.